Dave Bolt
Luckmore Bunu

Almost Human Publications

They would be giggling at Tom's silly jokes turning the day into a laugh-filled adventure.

Lars chuckled, "Tom, you're hilarious!"

Perched on a tree stump, Tom struck a dramatic pose, ready to unveil something extraordinary. Lars and Liam, wide-eyed and eager, anticipated the impending excitement.

"Get ready, pals! This is going to be epic!" Tom proclaimed.

"Investing? What's that?" Liam asked, eyes wide with curiosity.

"It's like making money work for you. Let me show you," Tom explained.

In Tom's room, he proudly showcased his clandestine piggy bank treasure. "This is where I stash my savings from my profits, my friends!" Lars and Liam were awestruck - a treasure trove of money in one place!

"Whoa, Tom, that's a fortune!"

Tom shared how he earned extra money on his uncle's avocado farm during holidays,

BUSINESS

"That's a stock!" he explained, making the stock market sound like an exhilarating secret.

"A stock? Like, from the store?" Liam asked, a bit perplexed.

"No, it's like owning a slice of the pie that the whole company bakes," Tom clarified. Lars and Liam were astounded by the enchantment of the stock market, their eyes filled with wonder as Tom unraveled the mysteries of investing.

"Wait, you mean, you can own a piece of a big company?" Lars gasped.

"And as the company grows, so does the value of your piece," Tom added.

"I want my piggy bank to be as awesome as Tom's!" Liam declared.

"And remember, it's not just about saving but making your money work for you," Tom reminded them.

In the candy shop, Liam, piggy bank in hand, bravely turned down the sweets, learning to resist those tempting impuls

Tom guided his friends on creating a budget and resisting the allure of treats and toys.

Like a roadmap for their financial journey

"Okay, guys, let's plan. Budgets are like treasure maps," Tom suggested.

"And every coin you save is a step closer to discovering the treasure," Lars added.

"I really want those candies, but I gotta save and invest," Liam sighed.

"You're investing in your future success by making smart choices now," Tom encouraged.

Tom Said, "Hey guys let's also invest in our own small business!

But what business? All at once the boys said "ICE CREAM" and that was it! Game on!

Now in the kitchen, the trio transformed ingredients into dreams, whipping up homemade ice cream. Laughter echoed as their simple idea turned into a delectable adventure.

"I hope people love our ice cream flavors," Lars chuckled.

"And every scoop sold is a sweet return on our investment of time and effort," Tom pointed out.

Setting up an ice cream stand in the neighborhood was a thrilling adventure. The line stretched down the block as people raved about their delectable treats.

Tom, Lars, and Liam couldn't help but feel a sense of accomplishment. As they counted their profits at the end of the day, the sun dipping below the horizon painted the sky in hues of orange and pink. Tom, with a satisfied grin, exclaimed,

"Look at what we've accomplished, guys! This is just the beginning."

Lars, still savoring the success, chimed in, "Who would've thought our homemade ice cream would be such a hit?

Liam, carefully counting the coins, added, "And it's not just about the money. It's about the joy we brought to people's faces."

Tom nodded, "Exactly! Our little ice cream venture taught us about more than just profit. It's about creating something, sharing it with others, and enjoying the journey."

The trio discussed their dreams for the future. Lars, looking into the distance, said.

"Imagine having our own ice cream truck, traveling around, spreading happiness and deliciousness everywhere, and making huge bank as we invest our profits!"

Liam, excited, exclaimed, "And maybe we can introduce new flavors, like chocolate chip cookie dough swirl with a sprinkle of financial wisdom!"

Tom laughed, "I love that idea, Liam! Who knows, maybe one day we'll have a whole ice cream empire."

Meet Luckmore Bunu, a community pharmacist with a passion for storytelling that goes beyond the pharmacy counter. Armed with a B Pharm Hons from UZ and an MSc from Liverpool, he is currently on a journey to add a Professional Certificate in General Dermatology from Australia to his list of accomplishments.

As a loving father to one daughter, Luckmore's connection with children extends beyond his professional life. In the enchanting world of children's literature, he crafts tales that captivate young minds. Beyond the world of whimsical narratives, Luckmore delves into the exciting realm of retail investment, navigating ASX, VFEX, and ZSE with the curiosity of an adventurer. His investment journey began in the last quarter of 2021, and since then, he has immersed himself in pages of financial information. In addition, he has dedicated hours to absorbing insights from various investment seminars, workshops, and talks.

Drawing inspiration from legendary investors like Warren Buffett and the late Charlie Munger, Luckmore infuses his storytelling with lessons that extend beyond the pages of his books. When he's not spinning tales or navigating the financial markets, he finds joy in the simple pleasures of writing, traveling to new realms, and engaging in heartwarming conversations.

Contact Luckmore on bunu.luckmore@gmail.com

Meet Dave Bolt – a talented illustrator and a devoted father of three. With a passion for creativity and years of experience, Dave has been creating illustrations and working as a youth worker.

As a parent, Dave appreciates the magic of storytelling combined with the imaginative minds of children.

His experiences at home inspire him to create illustrations that capture the hearts and minds of young readers.

In addition to his role as an illustrator, Dave has a background as a youth worker, where he connects with and guides the younger generation. His blend of artistic talent and understanding of young minds makes him stand out in the world of children's literature. Dave enjoys collaborating with emerging writers, turning their stories into visually appealing works of art. His aim is not just to create illustrations but to make stories unforgettable for readers of all ages. Beyond illustration, Dave extends creativity to schools and groups through engaging cartooning and publishing workshops. With mentoring and motivational speaking services, Dave shares his experiences, inspiring others to explore their potential.

To connect with Dave and explore creativity, visit his website at www.davebolt.com.au. For inquiries, email him at dave@davebolt.com.au or call him at +61 402419131. Join Dave Bolt in embracing the power of imagination and creativity – where every page is a canvas waiting to be filled with wonder!

www.ingramcontent.com/pod-product-compliance
Lightning Source LLC
Chambersburg PA
CBHW041712290426
44109CB00028B/2855